ADVANCING THE KINGDOM

GOD'S PLAN FOR REDEEEMING HIS CREATION

HAMP LEE III

Copyright © 2014, 2018 by Hamp Lee III.

All rights reserved. No part of this publication may be reproduced, distributed or transmitted in any form or by any means, including photocopying, recording, or other electronic or mechanical methods, without the prior written permission of the publisher, except in the case of brief quotations embodied in critical reviews and certain other noncommercial uses permitted by copyright law. For permission requests, write to the publisher at info@commissionpubs.com.

All scripture references used in this book are from the KING JAMES BIBLE.

Cover photo courtesy of Pearl.

Advancing the Kingdom/ Hamp Lee III – 2nd ed.
ISBN 978-1-940042-59-6

Jerome, I greatly appreciate our talks on the Kingdom of God. Our conversations were the catalyst for this book.

Contents

Introduction	7
Overview of the Bible	11
A Kingdom Lost	15
A Coming Kingdom	21
The King Has Come	23
The Kingdom of God	29
Cost of the Kingdom	37
Living for the Kingdom	41
Conclusion	45

Introduction

My heart was racing. I was scared. I stood up in the midst of the church and walked to the front. The pastor offered the gift of salvation to anyone that was in need and I felt compelled to accept his invitation.

When I came forward, I was welcomed by the pastor and two others standing with him. As I stood in front of the pastor, he asked me several questions: did I believe Jesus Christ was the Son of God; did He die for my sins; did Jesus rise from the dead after three days; and if He sits on the right hand of God making intercession for me. Though it was the first time I had ever heard these questions, I answered yes to each one. I did not understand what was going on or what was to come next. I only wanted to become a Christian.

The church I was attending did not have a new believer's class, so I attended as many weekly services as possible. As time went on, my understanding of the bible grew and I became more confident in my studies.

Almost fifteen years later, I had the honor of serving as a church pastor. As I stood in the front of the church offering the gift of salvation, I felt compelled to help others gain a greater understanding of the bible and God's plan for His creation. And this was my purpose for writing *Advancing the Kingdom*.

If Christianity is new to you, I would ask that you study *Advancing the Kingdom* with at least one other person that is familiar with the bible. When I started out, there were so many things I did not understand about Christianity, and having a friend to help me along the way was beneficial. He was able to explain specific terms and scriptures I did not understand. If you do not have a close friend who is knowledgeable about the bible, please contact me using the e-mail or website address at the back of the book.

Additionally, it will be important for you to find a suitable bible. There are many bible versions translated from the original languages of Hebrew, Aramaic, and Greek. Some bible versions are meant for greater readability while others are focused on literal translations from the original languages.

With so many bible versions, it might seem like a daunting task to select the best one for you. The first time I went to a bookstore to purchase a bible, the ten-foot wall of bibles overwhelmed me. I did not know the difference between any of them. Thankfully, I was with a friend that helped me find a bible that was tailored to my needs as a new believer.

Regardless of the bible version you use, please take your time to digest the contents of this book. Though this book may seem small, *Advancing the Kingdom* is packed with scriptural references on almost every page. Research every reference and statement for your personal growth and edification.

The bible is the most important book ever written, telling the most important story ever shared with mankind. Therefore, I pray *Advancing the Kingdom* will help you understand God's message to His creation and will be one of your companions for growing into the man or woman God has always intended you to be.

Overview of the Bible

The bible is a collection of sixty-six separate books divided into the Old and New Testament. The Old Testament encompasses thirty-nine books and the New Testament twenty-seven books. Each book shares a perspective of God's message, purpose, and will. Some books are only historical references, while others are for all people to follow and obey. The following pages highlight the contents of the Old and New Testament:[1]

OLD TESTAMENT
The Pentateuch—*Genesis, Exodus, Leviticus, Numbers, and Deuteronomy*

The Pentateuch, which means "five vessels or containers," are the first five books of the bible. They describe the creation of the earth and man, the nation of Israel, and Israel's covenant and laws.

---

[1] "Books of the Bible :: Study the Divisions of the Books of the Bible." About.com Christianity. Web. 19 May, 2014. http://christianity.about.com /od/booksofthebible/tp/Books– Of–The–Bible.htm.

Historical Books—*Joshua, Judges, Ruth, 1 and 2 Samuel, 1 and 2 Kings, 1 and 2 Chronicles, Ezra, Nehemiah, and Esther*

The historical books describe the history of the people of Israel. They detail Israel's entry into their promised land and how they split into two kingdoms. They also testify of the Israelites' captivity and later return to their homeland.

Psalms and Wisdom Books—*Job, Psalms, Proverbs, Ecclesiastes, and Song of Songs*

The psalms and wisdom books describe praise, worship, poetry, instruction, songs, and intimacy. They show how love, intimacy, and wisdom can help people live a joyous and righteous life before God.

The Prophets—*Isaiah, Jeremiah, Lamentations, Ezekiel, and Daniel, Hosea, Joel, Amos, Obadiah, Jonah, Micah, Nahum, Habakkuk, Zephaniah, Haggai, Zechariah, and Malachi.*

The prophets describe the later years of the divided kingdoms of Israel and Judah. They speak of their period of captivity and later return to Israel.

NEW TESTAMENT
The Gospels—*Matthew, Mark, Luke, and John*

The Gospels describe the birth, life, teachings, death, and resurrection of Jesus Christ.

Acts

The book of Acts follows the history of the early church after the resurrection of Jesus Christ. It also describes the spread of Christianity throughout the known world.

The Epistles—*Romans; 1 and 2 Corinthians; Galatians; Ephesians; Philippians; Colossians; 1 and 2 Thessalonians; 1 and 2 Timothy; Titus; Philemon; Hebrews; James; 1 and 2 Peter; 1, 2, and 3 John; and Jude*

The epistles are letters written to many of the early churches and believers. Paul, an apostle of Jesus Christ and a former persecutor of the early church, wrote many of the epistles.[2]

---

[2] Acts 9:1–31.

Revelation

The book of Revelation is the revelation of Jesus Christ.[3] It contains prophetic messages written to describe the last days before the destruction of the earth, the punishment of the devil and his angels, and the final placement of those who are (and are not) listed in the Book of Life. It is the conclusion of God's message to His people and a message of hope for those who overcome sin and the world.

---

[3] Revelation 1:1.

A Kingdom Lost

God created the heavens and earth.[4] The earth was created as a place where man could dwell in eternal fellowship with God. Man was created in the image of God and for His glory.[5] Man and woman (Adam and Eve) were created without sin or the knowledge of good or evil—they were both naked and unashamed.[6] After creating man and woman, God told them to (1) have dominion over every living thing that moves upon the earth; (2) be fruitful, multiply, and replenish the earth; and (3) subdue it.[7]

God placed man in the garden of Eden to dress and keep it.[8] He gave Adam one commandment to follow: not to eat the fruit from the tree of the knowledge of good and evil. God said that if he ate of this fruit, he would surely die.[9]

---

[4] Genesis 1–2.

[5] Isaiah 43:1–7.

[6] Genesis 2:25.

[7] Genesis 1:26–29.

[8] Genesis 2:15.

[9] Genesis 2:17.

One of the creatures, the serpent, came to Eve in order to tempt her to eat the fruit from the tree of the knowledge of good and evil. The serpent is also known as Lucifer, the devil, and Satan.[10] Lucifer was an anointed being (cherub) that was once upon the holy mountain of God.[11] He was beautifully covered with every precious stone and was filled with pipes and tabrets (timbrels, tambourines) in the day he was created. He was perfect in all his ways until sin was found in him.

Lucifer's heart became lifted up because of his beauty. His wisdom was corrupted through the reason of his brightness. Lucifer sought to place his throne above the stars of God.[12] He enticed one-third of the angels in heaven to join him against God. For their actions, Lucifer and the angels that sided with him were removed from heaven and will be punished at a later date.[13]

Satan is a deceiver, tempter, and adversary against God and His creation.[14] Satan's name is defined as

---

[10] Isaiah 14:12–15; Revelation 12:9–10.

[11] Ezekiel 28:11–19.

[12] Isaiah 14:12–15.

[13] Ezekiel 28:16–19; Luke 10:18; Revelation 12:4, Revelation 20.

[14] Matthew 4:1–11; 1 Thessalonians 3:5; Revelation 12:9–10.

'adversary' and devil is defined as 'prone to slander, slanderous, accusing falsely.'[15]

As the serpent tempted Eve to eat the fruit, she saw how the tree was good for food, pleasant to the eye, and a tree to make one wise. She took the fruit from the tree and ate it. After eating, Eve gave some to Adam.[16] When Adam ate the fruit, both of their eyes were opened, gaining the knowledge of good and evil. Sin and death entered the world. They (and all people after them) would know murder, jealousy, anger, strife, and all manner of sin and desires of the flesh.

Wherefore, as by one man sin entered into the world, and death by sin; and so death passed upon all men, for that all have sinned

—Romans 5:12

When Adam and Eve realized they were naked, they sewed fig leaves together to cover themselves.[17] Because of his disobedience to God's command, Adam (and all mankind) would surely die, but there were other consequences.

---

[15] "Greek Lexicon :: G1228 (KJV)." Blue Letter Bible. Sowing Circle. Web. 16 Jan, 2014. http://www.blueletterbible.org/lang/lexicon/lexicon.cfm?Strongs=G1228&t=KJV.

[16] Genesis 3:1–11.

[17] Genesis 3:7.

First, the authority and dominion that God gave to man was now usurped by the devil. He became the prince of the power of the air and the god of the earth.[18] Though the devil has influence, dominion, and power on earth, his authority and power is limited by God.[19] He seeks to expand his dominion on earth by influencing people to live in opposition to God's standard.

Second, because of God's holiness, man could no longer be with Him forever.[20] Holiness is the epitome of God's nature and no sin can dwell with Him.[21] God hates sin as it ushers selfishness, evil, and separation from His purpose and will.[22]

Though separated from the man and woman He created, God loved them so much that He put a plan in motion that would destroy the works of the devil and restore the eternal position of man.[23] After God confronted Adam for his disobedience, He brought judgments upon the woman, serpent, and the earth.

---

[18] John 8, John 12:31; 2 Corinthians 4:1–4; Ephesians 2:2; Colossians 1:13; 1 John 5:19.

[19] Job 1:6–12, Job 2:1–7.

[20] Israel 59:1–2; Romans 5:12.

[21] Psalm 5:4.

[22] Psalm 89:35; Psalm 92:15; Isaiah 13:11; Jeremiah 5:25; Romans 9:14.

[23] Ezekiel 33:11; John 3:16; 2 Peter 3:9; 1 John 3:8.

God foretold that a seed of woman (a child) would crush the head of the serpent, while the serpent would bite the heel of the child.[24] The seed of woman would restore the eternal relationship between God and man.

---

[24] Genesis 3:14–15.

A Coming Kingdom

As the story of humanity continued, God established a nation of people for Himself through a man named Abraham—the people of Israel.[25] God stated that Abraham would be the father of many nations, and through him, all nations would be blessed.[26] As God established Israel as a nation, He became their king and ruler.[27] God established a covenant (contract) outlining specific instructions and judgments to govern their conduct.[28] The Israelites would represent His holy nature and standard among the other nations.

Within the covenant, God provided blessings for obedience and judgments for sin.[29] Though the people of Israel initially agreed to the conditions of the covenant, they would cycle through obedience and disobedience time and again. When the Israelites

---

[25] Genesis 12:1–4, Genesis 15.

[26] Genesis 22:18; Acts 3:25; Galatians 3:8.

[27] 1 Samuel 8:4–7.

[28] Exodus 20–Deuteronomy; Leviticus 26:9–12.

[29] Deuteronomy 27–28.

sinned against God, He provided instructions on how they were to atone for their sin—through the sacrifice of calves and goats.[30] In addition, each year the high priest over the Israelites would present himself before God to offer sacrifices for the sins of his life and the people. However, the sacrifices could not satisfy an eternal requirement for sin.

In addition to the provision of sacrifices for the sins of Israel, God also sent judges to deliver them when times of disobedience and sin brought hardship and affliction from their enemies.

In time, the Israelites no longer desired God as their king and wanted a human king like the neighboring countries.[31] God fulfilled their request and declared that through Israel's second king, David, his kingdom would be without end.[32] God also announced that a son would be born that would rule over the people forever.[33]

---

[30] Leviticus 4–6.

[31] 1 Samuel 8–11.

[32] 2 Samuel 7:11–16; Jeremiah 23:1–6; Luke 1:30–33; Galatians 3:6–29.

[33] Isaiah 9:6–7; Luke 1.

The King Has Come

The bible declares that God loved the world (His creation) so much that He sent His Son Jesus. The name Jesus originates from a Hebrew word which means Jehovah (God) is salvation.[34] God became a man and dwelt among us.[35]

God became a man in order to save His creation from sin. Jesus' sacrifice would restore the eternal relationship between God and man.[36] He foretold a sign would be given concerning Jesus' birth: a virgin being found with child would give birth to a son:[37]

For unto us a child is born, unto us a son is given: and the government shall be upon his shoulder: and his name shall be called Wonderful, Counsellor, The

---

[34] "Greek Lexicon :: H3091 (KJV)." Blue Letter Bible. Sowing Circle. Web. 1 Oct, 2016. https://www.blueletterbible.org/lang/lexicon/lexicon.cfm?Strongs=H3091&t=KJV. Jesus received His name by inheritance from God (Hebrews 1:1–4). Jesus is the fulness of the Godhead bodily (Colossians 2:9): *For there are three that bear record in heaven, the Father, the Word, and the Holy Ghost: and these three are one.*—1 John 5:7

[35] Matthew 1:23; John 1:1, 14; Acts 20:28.

[36] John 3:16–17; Philippians 2:5–11; 1 Timothy 2:3–4; Titus 3:4–6.

[37] Isaiah 7:14, 9:6, 40:1–5; Matthew 1:18–25.

mighty God, The everlasting Father, The Prince of Peace.

—Isaiah 9:6

There are two reasons why Jesus was born of a virgin. First, Jesus is the Son of God. When Jesus was conceived, He was not born of a man and woman but the Holy Spirit. The Holy Spirit came upon the virgin and the power of the Most High overshadowed her. She was then found with child.[38]

The second reason why Jesus is born of a virgin is that the sin of Adam is passed through the man, not the woman. Adam was specifically told not to eat the fruit from the tree of the knowledge of good and evil.[39] As Jesus was not born through a man, He was born without the sin that originated from man.

Jesus is the seed of woman mentioned in Genesis 3:14–15. He is the son that would become the king of the eternal kingdom, as He is a descendent of the family line of David, the second King of Israel.[40] Through Jesus' life and perfect sacrifice, He restored the eternal relationship between God and man.[41]

---

[38] Luke 1:26–38.

[39] Genesis 2:16–17, Genesis 3:1–7.

[40] Isaiah 9:6–7; Matthew 1:18–25; Luke 1:26–38.

[41] Acts 13:38–39; Romans 3:25–26; Colossians 1:15–20, Colossians 2:13; Hebrews 4:15; 1 Peter 2:21–24; 1 John 2:1–2, 1 John 4:10.

Throughout Jesus' ministry on earth, He shared many things about the Kingdom of God. He provided food for the hungry, deliverance from affliction, teachings and commands for His followers, and was a servant to the masses of people around Him every day. Jesus' ministry highlighted two purposes for His coming:

1. Destroy the works of the devil.

The devil gained dominion (rule) of the earth by deceiving man. Though man once had dominion over the earth, all power and authority in heaven and earth had been given to Jesus.[42] If Satan was able to deceive Jesus, he could gain control of heaven and earth and accomplish his goal of establishing his throne above the stars of God.[43]

When given an opportunity, the devil tempted Jesus after He was led by the Spirit into the wilderness for forty days and forty nights.[44] Though the devil tempted Him, Jesus did not give into his temptations and did not sin. Because Satan could not deceive

---

[42] Daniel 7:13–14; Matthew 9:6, Matthew 11:27, Matthew 28:18–20; John 3:35, John 5:27, John 13:3; John 17:1–4; Acts 2:36; Romans 14:9; 1 Corinthians 15:27; Ephesians 1:9–12; Ephesians 1:15–23; Philippians 2:5–11; Colossians 2:9–12; Hebrews 1:1–4; Hebrews 2:9–10; 1 Peter 3:18–22.

[43] Isaiah 14:12–15; Mark 12:1–11.

[44] Matthew 4:1–11.

Jesus, he decided to destroy Him through death. However, the devil did not know that Jesus' death was a part of God's plan.[45] This plan was a mystery from the beginning.[46] In His death, Jesus would destroy the works of the devil and usher salvation to mankind.

Forasmuch then as the children are partakers of flesh and blood, he also himself likewise took part of the same; that through death he might destroy him that had the power of death, that is, the devil; And deliver them who through fear of death were all their lifetime subject to bondage. For verily he took not on him the nature of angels; but he took on him the seed of Abraham. Wherefore in all things it behoved him to be made like unto his brethren, that he might be a merciful and faithful high priest in things pertaining to God, to make reconciliation for the sins of the people. For in that he himself hath suffered being tempted, he is able to succour them that are tempted.
—Hebrews 2:14–18

---

[45] John 12:12–36.

[46] 1 Corinthians 2:6–8.

2. To save sinners.[47]

Though man received the punishment of death and separation from God through the sin of Adam, God loved the world so much that He gave His own Son as a ransom to save many.[48]

Jesus' sacrifice was unlike those made under the covenant with the people of Israel. Where the Israelites made daily and yearly sacrifices to cleanse themselves from sin, Jesus' sacrifice would be an eternal sacrifice for the redemption of mankind, once and for all.

But Christ being come an high priest of good things to come, by a greater and more perfect tabernacle, not made with hands, that is to say, not of this building; Neither by the blood of goats and calves, but by his own blood he entered in once into the holy place, having obtained eternal redemption for us. For if the blood of bulls and of goats, and the ashes of an heifer sprinkling the unclean, sanctifieth to the purifying of the flesh: How much more shall the blood of Christ, who through the eternal Spirit offered himself without spot to God, purge your conscience from dead works to

---

[47] Luke 4:18–19, Luke 9:56, Luke 19:10; Acts 10:38; 1 Corinthians 15:22–26; 1 Timothy 1:15.

[48] Matthew 20:28; John 3:16–17; 1 Timothy 2:4–5.

serve the living God? And for this cause he is the mediator of the new testament, that by means of death, for the redemption of the transgressions that were under the first testament, they which are called might receive the promise of eternal inheritance.

—Hebrews 9:11–15

Jesus was sentenced to die by crucifixion and on the third day after His death, He rose from the dead to be the first of many to enter into eternal life.[49] Jesus now sits on the right hand of God's throne praying for you and me.[50]

---

[49] Matthew 26–28; Romans 8:29; Colossians 1:9–20.

[50] Isaiah 53; Matthew 20:17–19; Mark 16:19; Ephesians 1:3–7; Hebrews 9:27–28.

The Kingdom of God

The Kingdom of God represents the rule and realm of God. The Kingdom of God exists in two places. On earth, the Kingdom of God exists within you.[51] In eternity, there will be a new heaven, earth, and Jerusalem.[52]

In order to enter the Kingdom of God, you must be born again. Jesus stated that being born again is being born of water and the Spirit.[53] In being born of water and the Spirit, a person believes in Jesus, repents of his or her sins, is baptized, and receives the gift of the Holy Spirit.

---

[51] The Kingdom of God lives in you through the Holy Spirit (Luke 17:20–21). Some translations of Luke 17:21 state the Kingdom of God is in the midst of the Pharisees because Jesus is in their presence. In reading John 14:15-18 and 1 John 5:7, as the Holy Spirit lives in you and Jesus is one with the Father and Holy Spirit, where Jesus is, so is the Kingdom of God.
[52] Revelation 21:1–4, 22:1–5.
[53] John 3:1–8.

Believe in Jesus[54]

Everyone who believes in Jesus will be saved from the curse of sin and death and be given everlasting life.[55] This is the promise God gave to Abraham—that all nations through him would be blessed.[56] Jesus is the promised Messiah that came to redeem man from their sins.[57]

But not as the offence, so also is the free gift. For if through the offence of one many be dead, much more the grace of God, and the gift by grace, which is by one man, Jesus Christ, hath abounded unto many. And not as it was by one that sinned, so is the gift: for the judgment was by one to condemnation, but the free gift is of many offences unto justification. For if by one man's offence death reigned by one; much more they which receive abundance.

—Romans 5:15–17

---

[54] John 1:12, John 3:14–18, John 5:24, John 3:36, John 6:35, John 6:47, John 12:46; Acts 10:43; Acts 11:17–18, Acts 16:1–34; Romans 9:33, Romans 10:9–10; 1 Peter 2:6; 1 John 5:5–13.

[55] John 3:16–17.

[56] Genesis 22:18; Acts 3:25; Galatians 3:8.

[57] 2 Samuel 7:12–16; Isaiah 9:6–7; Daniel 2:44; John 18:33–37; Hebrews 1:8–9.

Those who believe in Jesus will become a child of God and a joint heir with Jesus.[58] They will receive God's Spirit and laws through a new covenant that will govern their actions and conduct.[59]

When you believe in Jesus, you place your hope, trust, and faith in Him. You believe your salvation rests in Jesus and God is a rewarder of everyone that diligently seeks Him.[60]

Repent of Your Sins[61]

Peter said unto them, Repent, and be baptized every one of you in the name of Jesus Christ for the remission of sins, and ye shall receive the gift of the Holy Ghost. For the promise is unto you, and to your children, and to all that are afar off, [even] as many as the Lord our God shall call.

—Acts 2:38–39

Repentance is turning away from your sinful nature and conduct. Some people will include an

---

[58] John 3:16–17; Romans 8:14–17; Galatians 4:7; Ephesians 2:8–10; Titus 3:7.

[59] Jeremiah 31:31–34; Matthew 22:34–40, Matthew 28:18–20; John 13:34–35; John 16:13; Romans 8:1–17; Galatians 5:16–25, Galatians 6:2; Ephesians 1:13–14; James 2:17–26.

[60] Hebrews 11:6.

[61] Matthew 4:17; Mark 1:14–15; Luke 13:3; Acts 3:19–21, Acts 5:31, Acts 17:30; 2 Corinthians 7:10

internal or external (vocal) confession to God.[62] You can repent in the midst of a crowded church or in the privacy of your home. When you repent of your sins, you turn to God where your actions become consistent with such repentance—righteousness, goodness, and truth.[63]

Be Baptized[64]

Being born of water represents water baptism. Through baptism, you receive forgiveness of and liberty (remission) from your sins. Your sins are washed away.[65]

Know ye not, that so many of us as were baptized into Jesus Christ were baptized into his death? Therefore we are buried with him by baptism into death: that like as Christ was raised up from the dead by the glory of the Father, even so we also should walk in newness of life.

—Romans 6:3–4

---

[62] Psalm 32:5; Proverbs 28:13; 1 John 1:8–10.

[63] Acts 26:20; Galatians 5:22–25; Ephesians 5:8–9.

[64] The Greek word for baptize is 'baptizo,' which is to dip repeatedly, to immerse, to submerge (of vessels sunk), to cleanse by dipping or submerging, to wash, to make clean with water, to wash one's self, bathe, to overwhelm. Matthew 28:18–20; Mark 16:15–16; John 3:3–7; Acts 1:5; Romans 6:1–4; 1 Corinthians 6:9–11; Galatians 3:27; Colossians 2:12.

[65] John 3:1–8; Acts 2:38, Acts 22:3–16; 1 Peter 3:21.

Born of the Spirit[66]

God declared that He would pour out His Spirit upon all flesh.[67] In being born of the Spirit, you become a new creation as you are renewed through the Holy Spirit's washing of regeneration and given the gift of the Holy Spirit.[68] The Holy Spirit is given as a guarantee (or deposit) of your future inheritance of eternal life.[69]

Through the Holy Spirit, you will be empowered to live as a faithful witness and ambassador for Jesus Christ.[70] You will receive a new covenant that will be in your heart.[71] The Holy Spirit will live within you and guide you into all truth.[72] The Holy Spirit will

---

[66] John 1:12-13; 1 Corinthians 6:11; 2 Corinthians 5:17; Ephesians 1:13-14, 5:22-27; Titus 3:4-7; 1 Peter 1:22-25.

[67] Joel 2:28–32; Acts 2:17.

[68] The words 'gift' and 'baptism' of the Holy Spirit had been used interchangeably in Scripture (Acts 10–11:1–17). God may also delay someone from receiving the gift of the Holy Spirit (Acts 2:1–4, Acts 8:5–17). This delay is not a specific precedent in every instance and should be considered independently from other disciples. Each instance is based on God's intentional timing and will. Luke 11:13; John 3:3–8, John 7:37–39, John 14:15–16; Acts 2:38, 5:32; Titus 3:3–7.

[69] Ephesians 1:10–14.

[70] Matthew 28:18–20; Mark 16:15–18; Luke 4:1–14, Luke 24:49; Acts 1:4–8; Romans 8:26–27; 1 Corinthians 2; 2 Corinthians 5:20, 2 Corinthians 6:1–11; Galatians 5:22–25; Ephesians 5:18.

[71] Jeremiah 31:31–34; Matthew 26:28; Luke 22:20.

[72] Ezekiel 36:26–27; John 14:16–18.

also give spiritual gifts to certain believers in order to accomplish God's purpose and will.[73]

For we ourselves also were sometimes foolish, disobedient, deceived, serving divers lusts and pleasures, living in malice and envy, hateful, and hating one another. But after that the kindness and love of God our Saviour toward man appeared, Not by works of righteousness which we have done, but according to his mercy he saved us, by the washing of regeneration, and renewing of the Holy Ghost; Which he shed on us abundantly through Jesus Christ our Saviour; That being justified by his grace, we should be made heirs according to the hope of eternal life.
—Titus 3:3–7

As Jesus' citizens in the kingdom of God (disciples), you will live in accordance to His Word and will (His rule and authority), which He provides in the Gospels.

In God's appointed time, Jesus will return to the earth to redeem His people; sentence the devil and his followers to an eternal punishment; and present a new heaven and earth, where everyone listed in the

---

[73] 1 Corinthians 12:1–11.

Book of Life will dwell eternally.[74] Jesus has the victory over the devil, death, the grave, and sin![75]

---

[74] Psalm 110; John 14:2–3, John 14:28; Acts 1:1–11; Colossians 3:4; 1 Thessalonians 4:16–18; Hebrews 9:27–28; Revelation 20–21:1–4.

[75] 1 Corinthians 15:51–58; Revelation 17–19.

Cost of the Kingdom

Jesus identified His followers as disciples.[76] A disciple is a pupil or learner.[77] Disciples study and follow Jesus' teaching and example.[78] For those who desire to become a disciple, Jesus said that he or she must first count the cost of following Him:

And there went great multitudes with him: and he turned, and said unto them, If any man come to me, and hate not his father, and mother, and wife, and children, and brethren, and sisters, yea, and his own life also, he cannot be my disciple. And whosoever doth not bear his cross, and come after me, cannot be my disciple. For which of you, intending to build a tower, sitteth not down first, and counteth the cost, whether he have sufficient to finish it? Lest haply, after he hath laid the foundation, and is not able to finish it, all that behold it begin to mock him, Saying,

---

[76] Disciples were identified as Christians (of Christ, Christ–followers) in Acts 11:26. Mark 2:14–16.

[77] "Greek Lexicon :: G3101 (KJV)." Blue Letter Bible. Sowing Circle. Web. 16 Jan, 2014. http://www.blueletterbible.org/lang/lexicon/lexicon.cfm?Strongs=G3101&t=KJV.

[78] Matthew 11:25–30; John 13:14–16; 2 Timothy 2:3–4; 1 Peter 2:20–25.

This man began to build, and was not able to finish. Or what king, going to make war against another king, sitteth not down first, and consulteth whether he be able with ten thousand to meet him that cometh against him with twenty thousand? Or else, while the other is yet a great way off, he sendeth an ambassage, and desireth conditions of peace. So likewise, whosoever he be of you that forsaketh not all that he hath, he cannot be my disciple. Salt is good: but if the salt have lost his savour, wherewith shall it be seasoned? It is neither fit for the land, nor yet for the dunghill; but men cast it out. He that hath ears to hear, let him hear.

—Luke 14:25–35

The purpose of counting the cost of being a disciple is to consider the lifelong, faithful commitment to Jesus regardless of your life experiences and/or the path or purpose He has for your life. Jesus said that no one who puts his or her hand to the plow (moving forward toward the Kingdom of God and eternal life) and looks back (toward their previous life) is fit for the Kingdom of God.[79] In order to live a life that is fit for the Kingdom of God, you must live by faith.

---

[79] Luke 9:62.

Hebrews 11:1 says that faith is the substance of things hoped for and the evidence of things not seen. What is being hoped for is an eternal city prepared by God.[80] The city is the *substance* of faith.

The life experiences of many disciples will be varied based on God's will and purpose. In reading Hebrews 11, there will be some that will experience seasons of peace and prosperity and witness the grace and power of God.[81] But there may be others that will face significant hardships and afflictions, some because of their association with Jesus.[82]

Think not that I am come to send peace on earth: I came not to send peace, but a sword. For I am come to set a man at variance against his father, and the daughter against her mother, and the daughter in law against her mother in law. And a man's foes shall be they of his own household. He that loveth father or mother more than me is not worthy of me: and he that loveth son or daughter more than me is not worthy of me. And he that taketh not his cross, and followeth after me, is not worthy of me. He that

---

[80] Hebrews 11:14–16.

[81] Hebrews 11:32–35.

[82] Mark 13:9–13; 2 Timothy 3:12; Hebrews 11:32–38.

findeth his life shall lose it: and he that loseth his life for my sake shall find it.

—Matthew 10:34–39

This is why it is important to count the cost of your decision to follow Jesus as a disciple. A life of peace and prosperity is not guaranteed because you believe in Jesus. Being a disciple is not about making your marriage better, finding a spouse, or receiving a better job. These things may be given to you, but you must understand the full measure of being a disciple.[83]

Taking up your cross is accepting your life experiences (prosperity, peace, hardship, and/or affliction) and faithfully following Jesus as His disciple. This is the *evidence* of what cannot be seen in Hebrews 11:1—the actions of someone who believes in Jesus, places his or her complete trust in Him, and faithfully obeys His commands and directions for his or her life, regardless of experience or circumstance. This person understands that through his or her obedience and faithfulness, he or she will one day receive eternal life and enter the Kingdom of God.[84]

---

[83] Matthew 5:43–48.

[84] John 3:1–8; Romans 8:12–17; Galatians 5:16–26; Titus 3:3–8; Hebrews 11; 1 John 2:1–3:10, 1 John 4:7, 1 John 5:1–21; Revelation 21:3–4.

Living for the Kingdom

Living as a disciple is a life-long commitment. Disciples learn of Jesus and His commands and represent Him in word and deed.[85] Through a life of compassion (love), communion, community, and commission, disciples grow into faithful men and women—to the glory of God.

Compassion

Compassion is the foundation of a disciple's life with God and man. Your love for God must be your first and chief aim—loving Him with all of your heart, mind, and soul.[86] And along with your love for God, you must also love others as yourself. It is your love for others that identifies you as Jesus' disciple.[87]

Master, which is the great commandment in the law? Jesus said unto him, Thou shalt love the Lord thy God with all thy heart, and with all thy soul, and with all

---

[85] Matthew 11:28–30; John 13:1–17; 1 Peter 2:21–25; 1 John 2:1–11.

[86] Matthew 22:36–40.

[87] John 13:35.

thy mind. This is the first and great commandment. And the second is like unto it, Thou shalt love thy neighbour as thyself.

— Matthew 22:36–39

Communion

Communion with God is paramount in the life of a disciple. The word communion is translated from the Greek language as fellowship, association, intimacy, and joint participation.[88] A disciple's communion with God is manifested from his or her knowledge and love for Him.[89] Communion is seeking the beauty and wonder of God.[90] It is cultivated from a disciple's time with God in prayer,[91] meditation,[92] praise,[93] and worship.[94] The deeper his or her communion with God, the deeper his or her

---

[88] "Greek Lexicon :: G2842 (KJV)." Blue Letter Bible. Sowing Circle. Web. 16 Jan, 2014. http://www.blueletterbible.org/lang/lexicon/lexicon.cfm?Strongs=G2842&t=KJV.

[89] Deuteronomy 7:7–8; Matthew 22:36–40; Philippians 3:7–11; Colossians 1:3–17; 1 John 4:19.

[90] 2 Samuel 7:18; Psalm 24:6, Psalm 27:8–10, Psalm 105:1–5, Psalm 119:1–17; Psalm 123:1–2; Isaiah 30:18; Matthew 11:28–30; Luke 2:36–38; Acts 13:1–3; Hebrews 11:6.

[91] Psalm 65:2, Psalm 145.

[92] Psalm 1:1–3, Psalm 119:15; James 1:22–25.

[93] Psalm 100, Psalm 103, Psalm 150; Hebrews 13:15.

[94] 1 Chronicles 16:29; John 4:24.

commitment and depth of his or her ministry within the world.

Community

Collectively, disciples encompass a worldwide body of believers. The community of disciples is identified by a shared belief in Jesus.[95] Disciples often gather in smaller groups or fellowships, such as the local church, to encourage, teach, and support one another toward a lifestyle of holiness unto God.[96] Disciples are the representation of God and His love within the world.[97]

Commission

And Jesus came and spake unto them, saying, All power is given unto me in heaven and in earth. Go ye therefore, and teach all nations, baptizing them in the name of the Father, and of the Son, and of the Holy Ghost: Teaching them to observe all things whatsoever I have commanded you: and, lo, I am with you always, even unto the end of the world. Amen.

—Matthew 28:18–20

---

[95] 1 Corinthians 12:13.

[96] Acts 2:42–47; Ephesians 2, Ephesians 4:8–12.

[97] Matthew 22:36–40; John 13:35; Galatians 6:1–10; Philippians 2:1–11; Hebrews 13:1–2.

Disciples represent people from every culture, social status, and location around the world. Through the use of gifts, talents, acts of service, and miraculous signs and wonders, disciples are empowered and sent to places near and far to share God's love and message with the world.[98] Disciples partner in the history and plan of God to represent Him and display good works for His glory.[99]

---

[98] Acts 13:1–4, Acts 16:1–10.

[99] Psalm 119:133; Proverbs 3:5–6, Proverbs 16:9; Matthew 5:14–16; Romans 10:10–15; 2 Corinthians 5:20.

Conclusion

It is my solemn prayer that *Advancing the Kingdom* has provided you with a greater understanding about God, His purpose in redeeming mankind, and how you can live for Him. A disciple who lives his or her life for God is one of great worth and purpose. Whether you are new to Christianity or have been walking with God for many years, you are very important to God. He loves you and has given His only Son so you can live for His glory on earth and eternally with Him in peace.

For future reading and study, please consider the following two books from our library:

Living for the Kingdom: Teaching What Jesus Taught. *Living for the Kingdom* provides over one hundred lessons on the teachings and commands of Jesus as outlined from Matthew 28:18–20 in the previous chapter. Jesus' teachings and commands are the foundation for living as His disciple and part of our Great Commission throughout the world.

The Bible Study Blueprint: An Essential Guide for Studying God's Word provides four methods for studying passages of scripture in the bible. You will learn how to find a scripture's historical and personal context, conduct in-depth word searches, develop detailed outlines, and build personal profiles.

www.commissionpubs.com
info@commissionpubs.com

www.ingramcontent.com/pod-product-compliance
Lightning Source LLC
Chambersburg PA
CBHW070802050426
42452CB00012B/2462